Students

Level 7 – Turquoise

Helpful Hints for Reading at Home

The graphemes (written letters) and phonemes (units of sound) used throughout this series are aligned with Letters and Sounds. This offers a consistent approach to learning, whether reading at home or in the classroom.

HERE IS A LIST OF PHONEMES FOR THIS PHASE OF LEARNING. AN EXAMPLE OF THE PRONUNCIATION CAN BE FOUND IN BRACKETS.

Phase 5			
ay (day)	ou (out)	ie (tie)	ea (eat)
oy (boy)	ir (girl)	ue (blue)	aw (saw)
wh (when)	ph (photo)	ew (new)	oe (toe)
au (Paul)	a_e (make)	e_e (these)	i_e (like)
o_e (home)	u_e (rule, cube)		

Phase 5 Alternative Pronunciations of Graphemes			
a (hat, what)	e (bed, she)	i (fin, find)	o (hot, so, other)
u (but, unit)	c (cat, cent)	g (got, giant)	ow (cow, blow)
ie (tied, field)	ea (eat, bread)	er (farmer, herb)	ch (chin, school, chef)
y (yes, by, very)	ou (out, shoulder, could, you)		

HERE ARE SOME WORDS WHICH YOUR CHILD MAY FIND TRICKY.

Phase 5 Tricky Words			
oh	their	people	Mr
Mrs	looked	called	asked
could			

TOP TIPS FOR HELPING YOUR CHILD TO READ:

- Allow children time to break down unfamiliar words into units of sound and then encourage children to string these sounds together to create the word.
- Encourage your child to point out any focus phonics when they are used.
- Read through the book more than once to grow confidence.
- Ask simple questions about the text to assess understanding.
- Encourage children to use illustrations as prompts.

This book focuses on /u/ and the alternative pronunciations of its grapheme. It is a Turquoise level 7 book band.

Can you sort these words into two groups?
One group has u as in **unicorn**.
One group has u as in **pudding**.

bull

awful

human

tuba

pull

bush

stupid

Students are people who are educated on new things. If you have classes each week, whether with a teacher or on a computer, you are a student.

You do not have to stop being a student when you are an adult. You can keep being a student for as long as you want.

Some people think that being educated is so important that they spend several years getting a degree. A degree is proof that someone has been successful in a subject.

Degree

To help them get a degree, students may go to lectures. A lecture is a speech about a particular topic.

People who give lectures are experts in their subjects. Students often take notes so that they do not forget what the lecture is about. They will read their notes later to help them remember what was said in the lecture.

If students want to discuss a lecture, they might meet together on a campus. They can then compare their notes and go over points that people did not understand.

Campuses are shared spaces used by lots of students. Campuses are good places to find lots of people with shared interests.

Some campuses have places for students to relax when they are not at lectures. They may have students' unions that run events or clubs for students to take part in.

To get a degree, students must first graduate. To do this, they need high marks on exams. Lots of students put their full focus into exams when they come around.

Some exams may take place a few times a year or at each new unit of a curriculum. The curriculum is all the things that students will be instructed on. A unit is one part of the curriculum.

Exams come in different formats. Some students have to submit essays. Submit means to hand in. Some students have to demonstrate that they have picked up new skills in their subject, which they might do by playing a musical instrument.

If you are not sure what you will do in the future, that is OK. You have lots of time to think about it! Taking the right degree can be a good step in helping you to do the things you want to do in the future.

©2023 BookLife Publishing Ltd.
King's Lynn, Norfolk, PE30 4LS, UK

ISBN 978-1-80505-106-0

All rights reserved. Printed in China.
A catalogue record for this book is available
from the British Library.

Students
Written by Charis Mather
Designed by Lucy Otter

An Introduction to BookLife Readers…

Our Readers have been specifically created in line with the London Institute of Education's approach to book banding and are phonetically decodable and ordered to support each phase of the Letters and Sounds document.

Each book has been created to provide the best possible reading and learning experience. Our aim is to share our love of books with children, providing both emerging readers and prolific page-turners with beautiful books that are guaranteed to provoke interest and learning, regardless of ability.

BOOK BAND GRADED using the Institute of Education's approach to levelling.

PHONETICALLY DECODABLE supporting each phase of Letters and Sounds.

EXERCISES AND QUESTIONS to offer reinforcement and to ascertain comprehension.

CLEAR DESIGN to inspire and provoke engagement, providing the reader with clear visual representations of each non-fiction topic.

AUTHOR INSIGHT:
CHARIS MATHER

Charis Mather is a children's author at BookLife Publishing who has a love for reading and writing. Her studies in linguistics and experiences working with young readers have given her a knack for writing material that suits a range of ages and skill levels. Charis is passionate about producing books that emphasise the fun in reading and is convinced that no matter how much you already know, there is always something new to learn.

This book focuses on /u/ and the alternative pronunciations of its grapheme. It is a Turquoise level 7 book band.

Image Credits Images are courtesy of Shutterstock.com. With thanks to Getty Images, Thinkstock Photo and iStockphoto. Cover – Tom Wang, Matej Kastelic, Incombible, vladwel. 4–5 – Ground Picture, Monkey Business Images. 6–7 – Studio Romantic, Drazen Zigic. 8–9 – wavebreakmedia, SeventyFour. 10–11 – Rawpixel.com, Monkey Business Images. 12–13 – fizkes, Monkey Business Images. 14–15 – Monkey Business Images, Gatot Adri.